THIS BOOK BELONGS TO

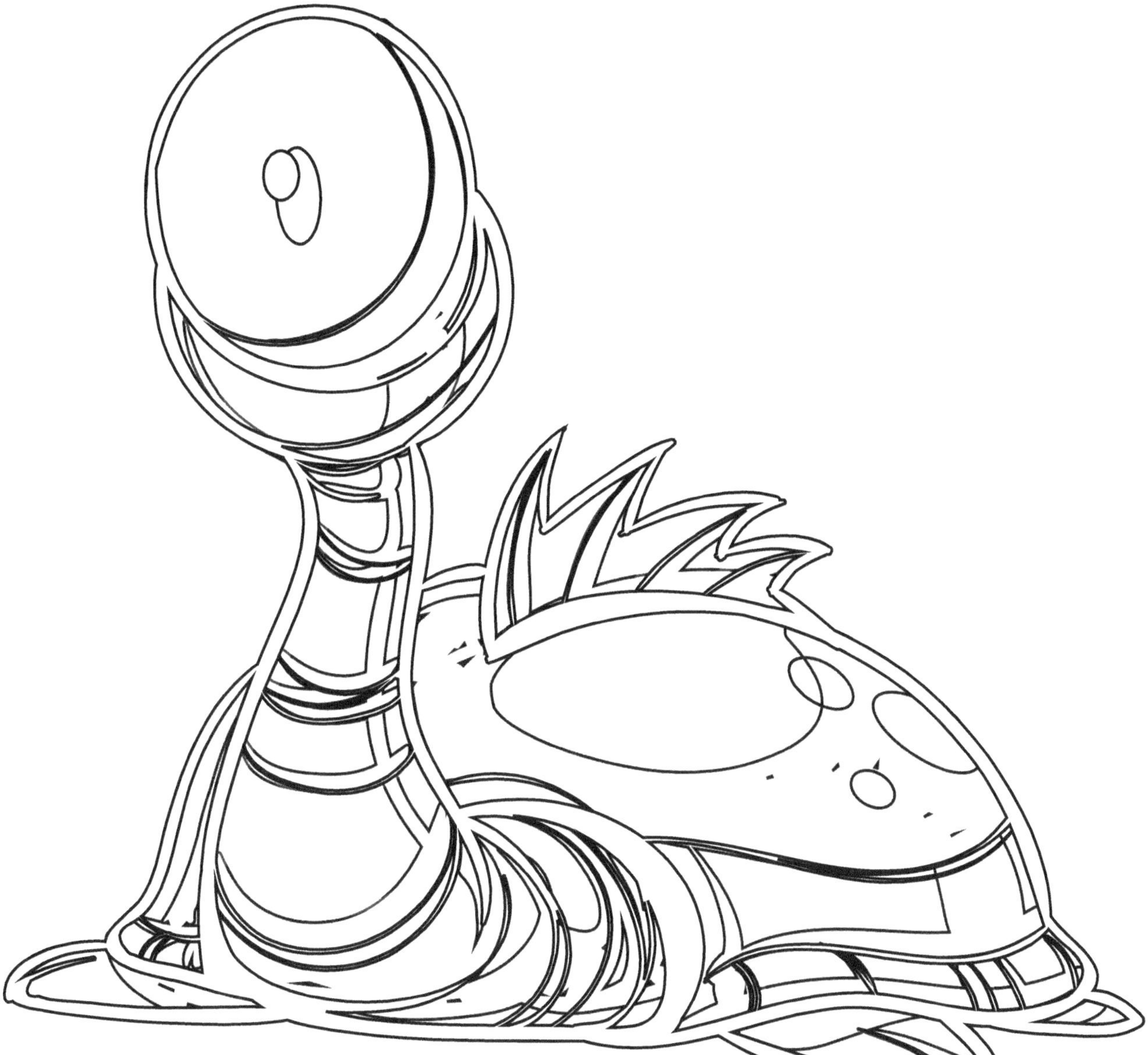

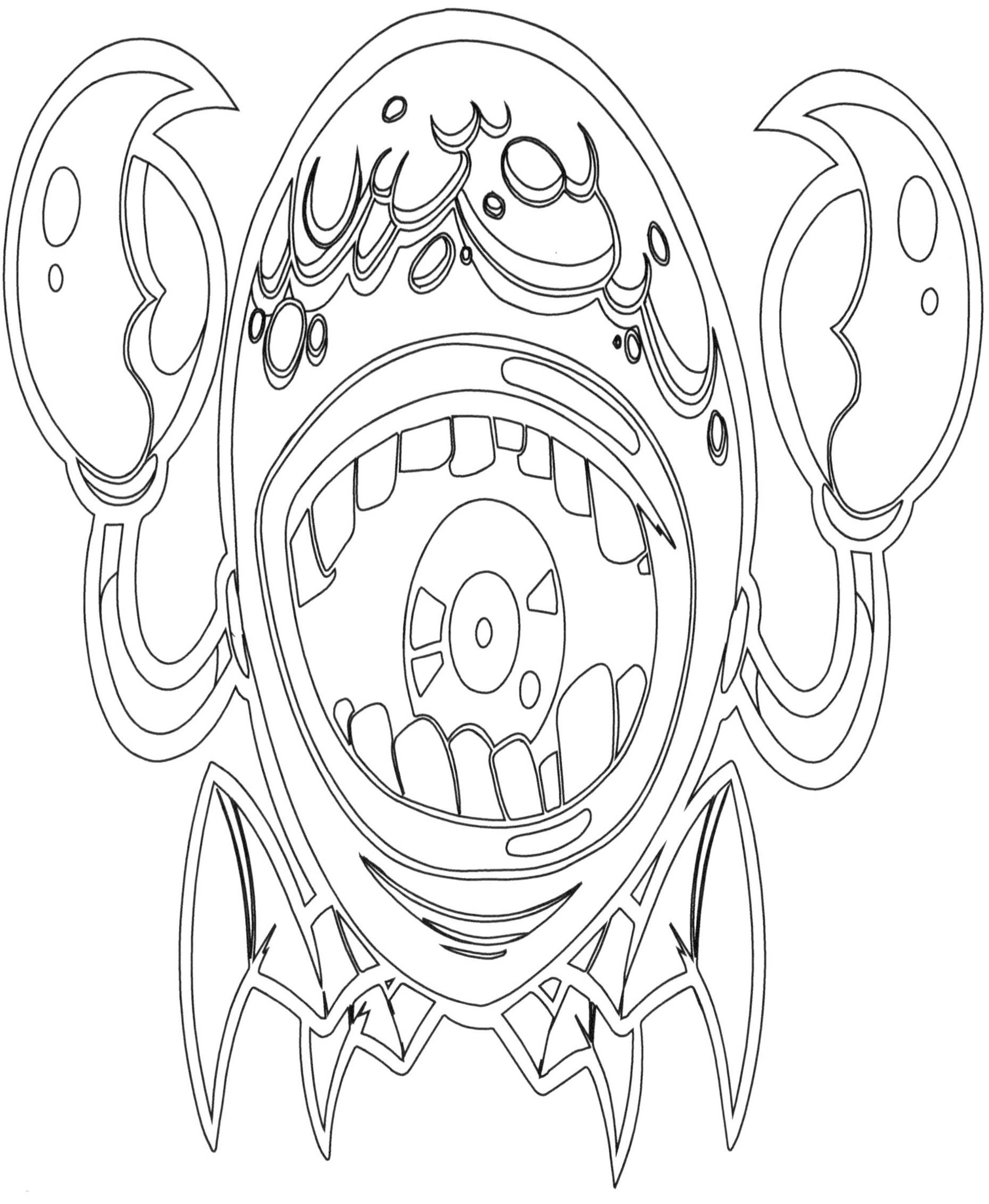

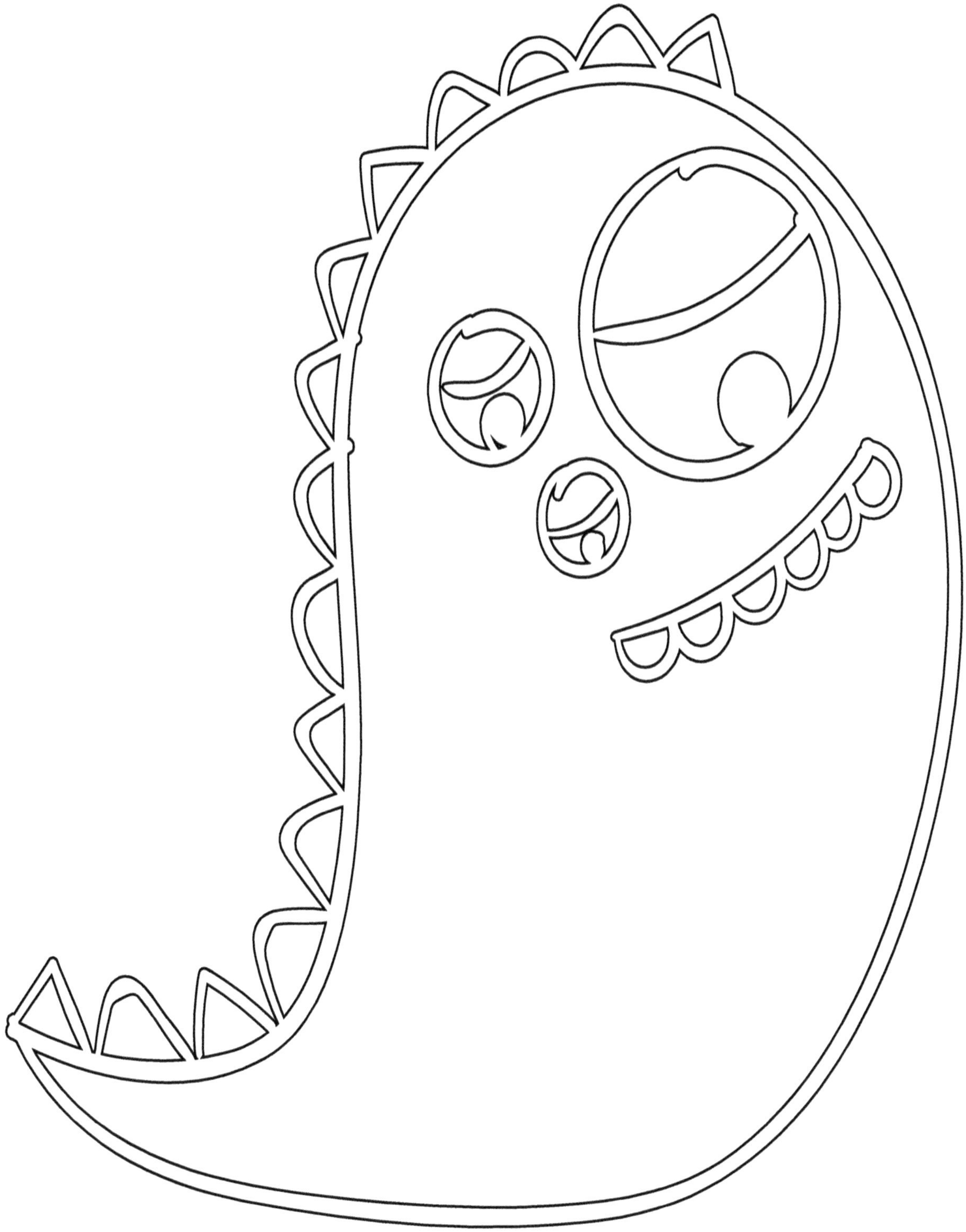

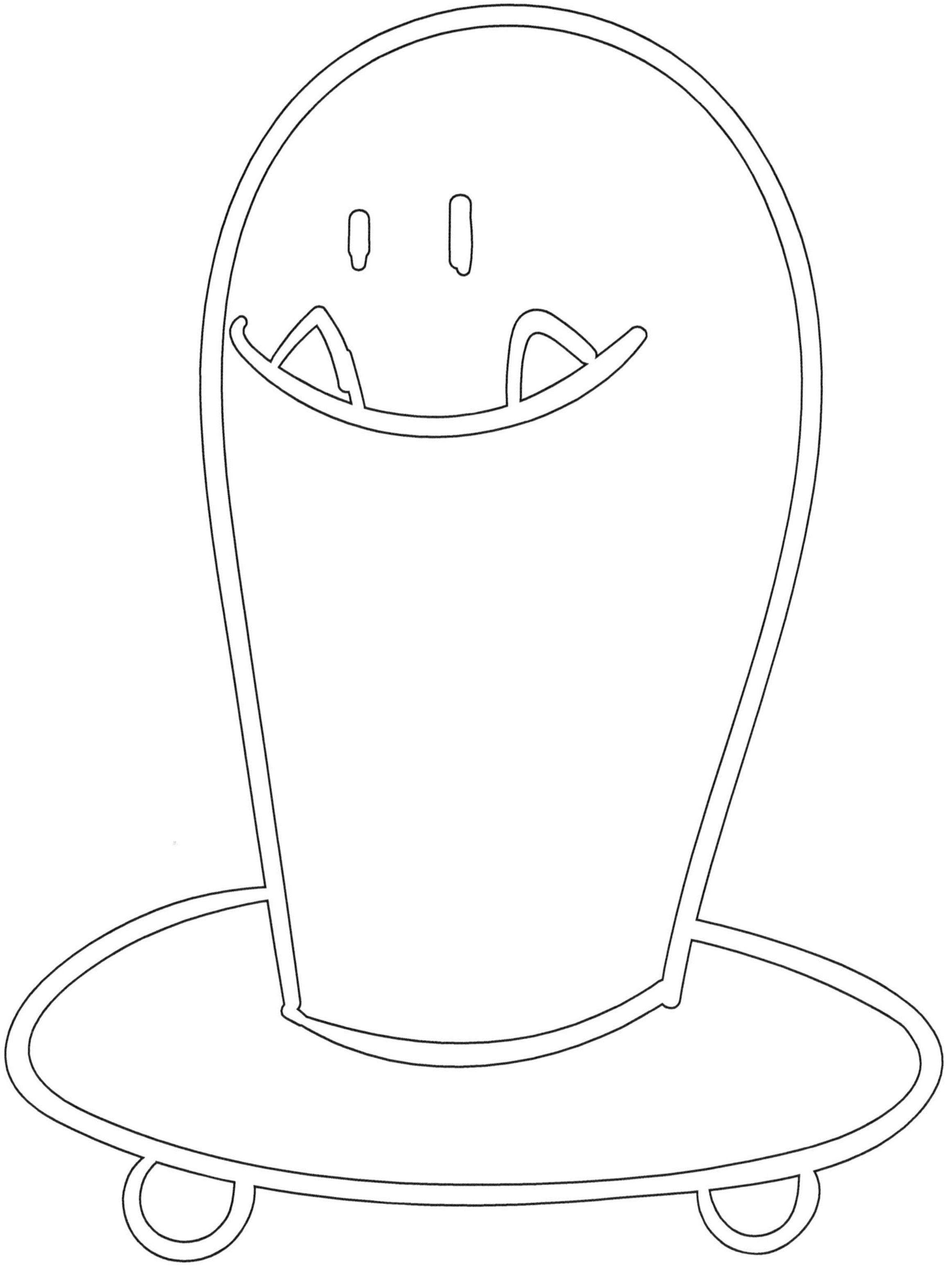

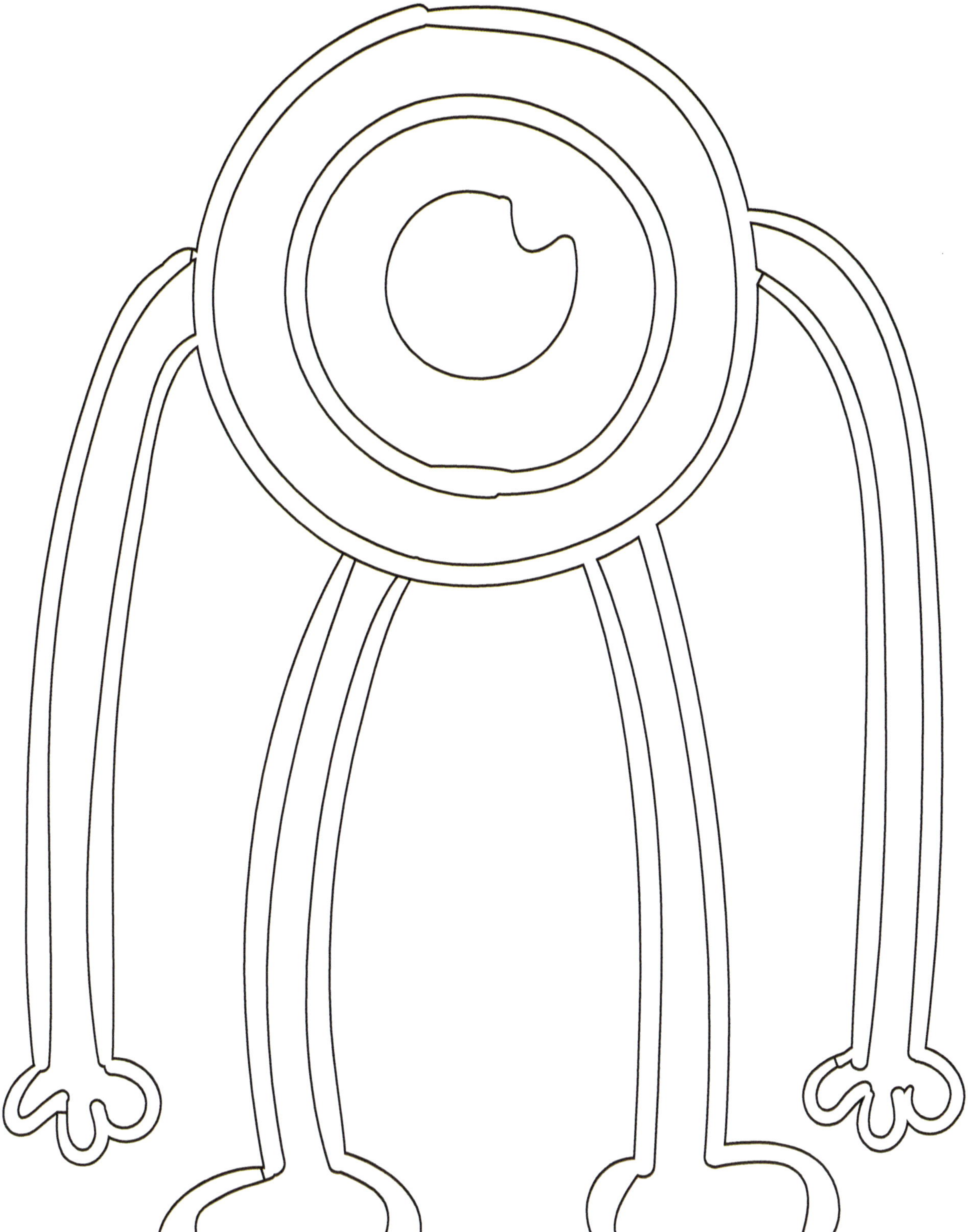

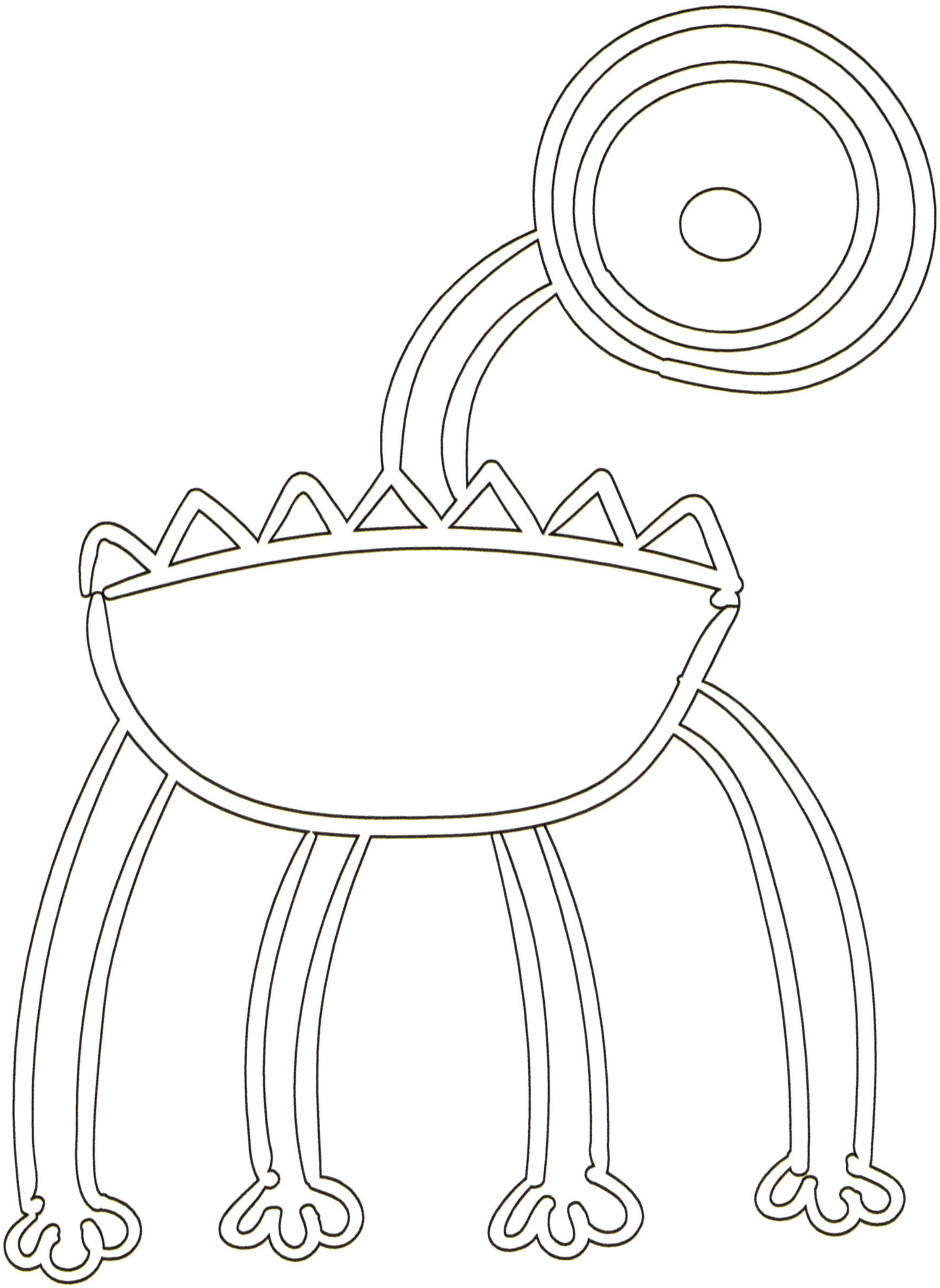

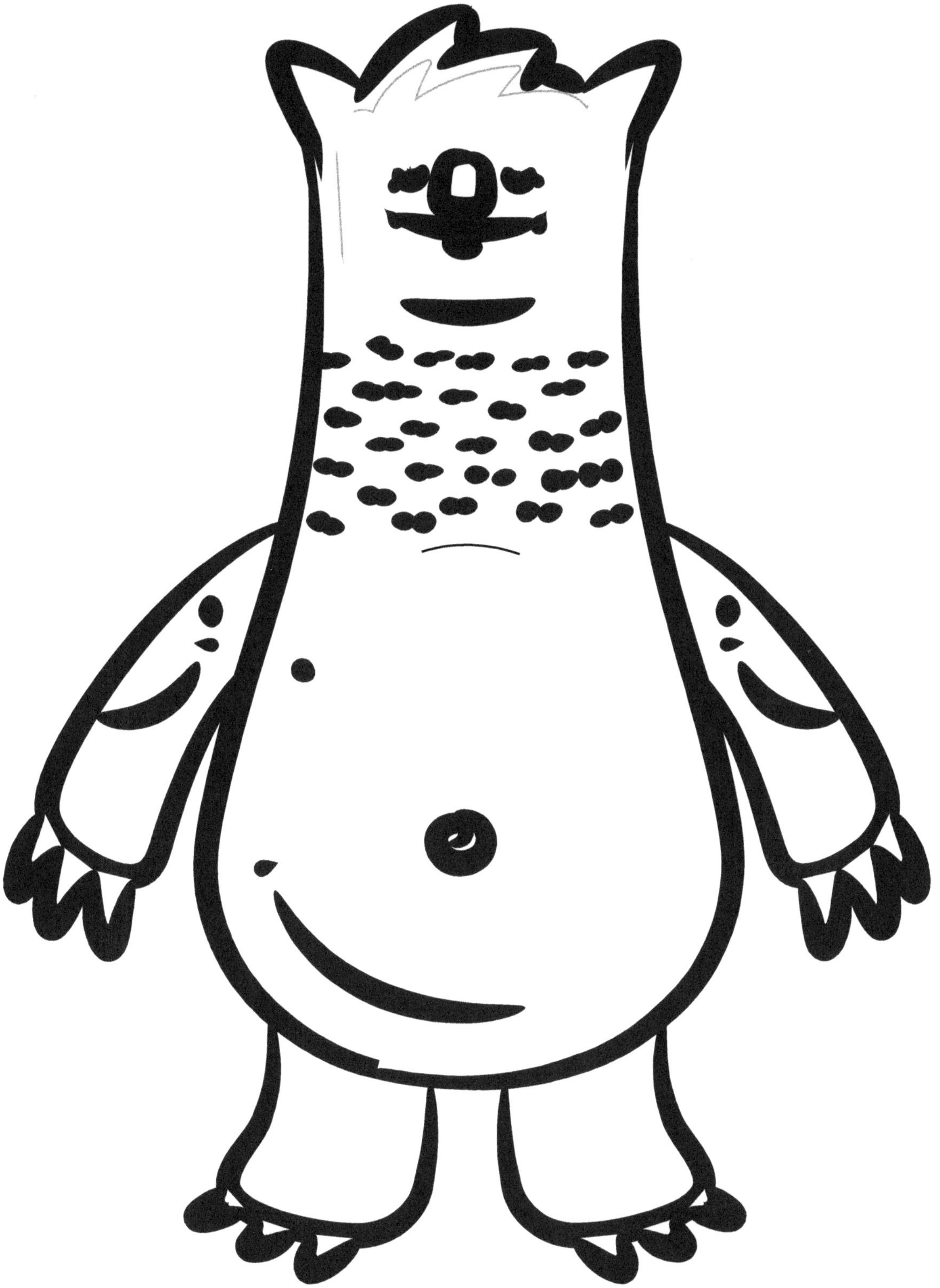

KIDS
IMAGINATION!

www.ingramcontent.com/pod-product-compliance
Lightning Source LLC
Chambersburg PA
CBHW080543060326
40690CB00022B/5208
* 9 7 8 1 7 9 9 1 9 1 0 7 0 *